10 Best World Most Expensive Fastest Exotic Cars

Best Sensational Unique Desktop Ultimate
One of Kind Reference Guide with Unique
Never Previously seen in One Publication
Pictures, Major Technical and Performance
Specifications for 10 World Best Exotic
High Performance Street Sport Cars

By Roman Slepyan

Special Edition

TABLE OF CONTENT

TABLE OF CONTENT(continued)

TABLE OF CONTENT(continued)

Foreword

1. History of cars

People were interested to travel, move in different ways without using their own energy and faster than to walk on feet by themselves from the ancient, prehistoric times. The animals like horses, elephants, camels were trained to carry people and cargo on the long distances. The use of horses to pull different kinds of carts, passenger carriages, cargo wagons were the usual business for 3000 years.

But in second half of 19th century the internal combustion engines made their way to transport people and cargo. The oldest among all internal combustion engines are the steam engines. They were too big to power the horseless wagons and carriages. The whole cycle of inventions had to happen in history and evolution of steam engines in order to transform them into current internal combustion engines as we know them now!   For 100 Years from the moment of "Invention" a car the people are very interested in fast moving horseless carriages and wagons in order to transport the passengers and cargo around the world to different destinations primary on short and middle distance local and regional routes. From the very start of car manufacturing the Car Design played the most important Role in sharpening the Car Image to create the long lasting and most favorable the First Impression on the News and Media and also the general public.

The news, media presents, sells and the general public accepts just the car body design as the Car Design in total! In the real life the car design could include much more than just the new more aerodynamic car body. The design of a new car includes the design of new engine, new transmission, new suspension, new steering, new accessories, new other car parts and assemblies.

Yes! The newly designed or redesigned exotic cars are presented to news and media to make into the breaking news by media announcements! The specialty concept cars are built by many car manufacturers to be displayed, introduced at the most prestigious world international auto shows with new body styles designs. It would cost the small fortune for car manufacturers to create and develop the concept of a new car from scratch! But there is the other side of car design. The car manufacturers want to display only their crown, most important achievements. And the mass-produced car would be quite different from the shiny concept newly designed cars by several reasons. The most important reason is to reduce as much as possible the costs to mass produce the new car in the hundreds thousands copies. The car engine design, body parts, other parts and assemblies' designs are mostly modified, revised to simplify the manufacturing by many different ways. The recent trend is to "borrow" the car engine design, body parts, car chassis, other parts and assemblies' designs from currently mass manufactured and assembled in the millions the makes and models of different cars. Car manufacturers want first of all to make the mass-produced car very cheap with lowest as possible expenses in total and manufacturing, technology costs in particular. It is not their priority any more to make each mass produced car to look exactly or very close like the shiny concept cars. Those mass produced in 100,000 and more copies new cars have the car body, car engine, transmission designs for the CHEAP manufacturing and reducing costs on technology use!

The Ford had manufactured 15 millions of Ford T car model during decades without big changes to car design and without adding new expenses to cost of manufacturing. His business model was to build and sell cars cheap that anybody with money could buy them without waiting. Current mass produced for millions buyers cars have the average speed and average car body design and sold to public at reasonable price! Another more unique and sophisticated car designs have been being used for 100 years to display the crown achievements by many best car manufacturers and to please the elite, royalty, celebrity's public, all those world famous and popular very eccentric rich, wealthy individuals. The exotic car manufacturers are building by hand labor the very unique prototypes cars and then would sell the limited very small number of copies from those prototypes to interested billionaires and movies' superstars actors. The unique and extreme car bodies design from carbon fiber and plastic reinforced hand made body panels creates unique car style and extreme sports car looks. The lowest weight of car body and other car parts and assemblies are used to minimize the waste of power distributed from a car engine to the driving wheels on the traction resistance between the car tires and the road under the smaller than made of metal car body the weight of the vehicle during propelling the car to unbelievably high Top speed. Such prototypes exotic sports cars have the unique engines designs like V12 or even W16 that present themselves by the design features as two V6 or two V8 installed together with rotation output to the one crankshaft in order to speed up cars at unbelievable strong and fast accelerations.

Foreword
2.History of unique fastest exotic cars

Price and amount of money to pay in order to own the unique exotic car never was the problem for richest people in the world! Their main problem in everyday life was and is now to make the statement about their money income, demonstrate the privileged and unique status and at same time to separate, make some distance and place themselves above all other people in "Crowd" of other car drivers on the street! And the ownership and driving of such one of kind unique cars would always confirm their exclusive status in human social hierarchy and would add some prestige to them with the automatic respect from the other drivers! The exotic cars are at the top of the Rich people's toys together with boats, mansions! Their Unique and privileged status should be reflected and perfected in everything they own or associated with! And business of manufacturing exotic extreme speeds toys is working as any other business. It has to be the demand from rich people to have such cars. The car manufacturer would just respond to received demand and build limited number of copies from their best unique prototypes. The new car manufacturing market was very crowded after the World War II. The relatively cheap American cars had got themselves the largest part of a world new car sales market. Some cars manufacturers from Italy and other Europe countries have chosen as their business to custom built by hands and sell the extreme exotic cars, often called the "dream machines" in limited quantities 20...400 cars with the implementing all latest hi-tech cutting edge automotive engines and cars design and technology, inventions and patents just because of this.

This only speed up and got world publicity in the late second half of 20th century while many the European car manufacturers struggled to survive in the competition with mass production cars in USA. Car manufacturers like Ferrari, Maserati, Lamborghini, Bugatti had to manufacture hand made cars with superior look, style and engine power! The top achievements for such hand made exotic cars are the top speed and most aerodynamic and funky looking fantastic futuristic exotic car body design. The top speeds could be achieved by using unique largest with measured in 1000 HP units of horse power Engines that would deliver the highest possible engine speed in RPM(rotation per Minute) and maximum possible 1000 lb-ft car engine torque. Those unique very lightweight materials to make the car body parts would make a whole car to weigh much less than regular cars with body parts from steel. The car engine would use the same amounts of power to accelerate a lightweight car to much higher top speeds. And those close to racing cars from Formula 1 the unique most aerodynamic futuristic exotic designs for car body are shaped to help make the losses of Engine Power to fight the resistance of air around the moving car as minimal as possible! It also contributes to much higher car top speeds!

Foreword

3. 10 Best World Fastest Exotic Cars-What is it?

The Author and Publishers of this awesome, fantastic and unique book are presenting to you the Top10 best fastest, exotic and most expensive street sports cars at the beginning of 21 Century! Now you own this fantastic book and the never published before the Automotive Top10 World Best Fastest Exotic Cars Mini Encyclopedia. Author had presented to you collected him the results of his extensive research inside this exclusive elite special report in form of book with pictures and all technical and performance specs for all top10 best fastest cars of all times! You will not find here built in quantities 1 or 2 for breaking the existing world top car speed records the experimental special cars with the rocket engines, or specialty built only for racing on the racing tracks the racing cars for the largest Formula1, GrandPrix, Le Mann, other car racing events! This book is totally about the street sports cars that everyone from the rich individuals with enough money could buy and drive without any "only racetrack use" restrictions every day and around the town! This book is different from the previously published book "Top10 List Fastest Most Expensive Exotic cars"
It is the much better special edition of same book with five times more never published before in one place information, more black and white pictures for each car, more unique knowledge and expertise! Author and Publishers are also preparing the Luxury Edition of this Book with more info on the Top 10World Best Fastest Exotic Sports Cars directly from Ferrari, Lamborghini, other exotic car manufacturers!

The luxury edition of this book comes with extra never published before in one place information, the full color pictures for each car, more unique knowledge and top expertise! As valued customer you could get exclusive advanced notice on publishing and release to mass distribution the luxury edition of this Book! Simply send email to streaminfobrokers@yahoo.com and subscribe to the Stream Info Brokers Mailing list.

This book and the luxury edition book would be the universal perfect gift for many individual and corporate holidays' and events' celebrations, many other occasions.

Introduction

Everybody and all People's Dream Car very easy could be one of the presented in this Awesome book World Top 10 Fastest Most Expensive Exotic cars! Those most sophisticated and technologically advanced models of cars ever to be designed, developed and built by hand at car manufacturer's facilities were presented to News, Media and General Public at Traditional Annual World largest International Auto Shows.

Every Rich Car Enthusiast could register and get on the waiting list for chance of their lifetime to buy one of the copies made from the displayed Exotic cars. However it is not guaranteed, that you will be the owner of such rare exotic cars. Each of exotic car manufacturers has always limited the quantity of prototype and small series cars for sale according to size of manufacturing facilities and the ability to finish build hand made cars during the one or 2, 3 years. Some manufacturers like Ferrari, Lamborghini would make available some more cheaper for limited mass manufacturing the car models in similar to exotic cars car bodies but with much smaller engine, cheaper transmission, brakes, other parts, assemblies and accessories. Such sales and distribution helped very much to make the Ferrari the popular car make, brand name and the typical household used name! Other manufacturers like Bugatti, Koenigsegg would prefer to build only prototype cars and sell each of them for millions each. They do not receive the recognition from car buyers just because of rarity of all manufactured for decades Bugatti and Koenigsegg cars.

The amounts of their hand made cars so small, that only the richest collectors would see, buy, own just one of them. The Car Price shown in this Book is the Manufacturer Suggested Retail Price or MSRP. There are no any new car dealers to take the delivery of new Ferrari cars straight from the Ferrari factory. All the new just manufactured exotic Bugatti, Maserati, Lamborghini, Mclaren FM1 cars were sold for some millions dollars directly from manufacturer to the individual car buyers by prepaid orders.

Introduction

You could see, buy and own presented in this unique
spectacular book the Exotic Makes and Models only as rare
Used Cars and only at the rare car auctions or from private
collections, when those "Toys" would change the owners
just because of limited total number of some models from
Ferrari, Maserati, Lamborghini, Mclaren.   Some of very
rich car enthusiasts, collectors, fans would get very lucky
to buy at auctions, or directly from private owners at much
higher "Collector" price those numbered top10 Best world
fastest exotic cars.   Other car enthusiasts and fans could
only dream about a ride inside or drive one of those "dream
machines."   Some very exotic cars would be from the
famous popular manufacturers like Ferrari, Lamborghini,
Mercedes-Benz, Porsche, that have been in this business
and built cars, exotic cars for 50 or more years. They
would quite regularly come up with new designs, concepts,
prototypes of new exotic cars good enough to be included in
the next top10 list of best fastest, expensive, exotic cars.
Other cars' Manufacturers like Audi, Chevrolet, Dodge,
Shelby for all their history had come up only with the 1 or 2
Exotic cars close to be presented in 10 Best Exotic cars List.
All Presented in this book super cars are legal to drive on the
city streets. But 55mph highways speed and 35mph street
speed limits are the official legal restrictions by law to the
car enthusiasts and exotic car drivers.   The unofficial street
races are illegal everywhere. Only the driving on the car
race track could satisfy the exotic car enthusiasts in feeling
the performance of their dream machines.

Each and every of top10 presented in this spectacular book exotic cars has same real life car body, car engine and drive train design as every Formula 1, GrandPrix and Le Man racing car. Such racing Mid-Engine/RWD Car Body Design Layout would make everyone behind the steering wheel of any of top10 exotic cars to feel like famous race car driver. Those rear wheel drive (RWD) exotic muscle cars require very different driver skills to drive them, than front wheel drive (FWD) mass produced the Toyota Corrola, Honda Civic cars.

Introduction

The author and well known car industry guru presents you here in this spectacular book with the never published before in printed or online publications the best final results of his extensive research on the rare exotic cars design, the performance and technical specifications for the world's best top10 fastest, most expensive exotic super cars.
You could stop now to waste your priceless time on doing yourself the research on 10 Best Exotic cars! Just relax, enjoy life pleasures, live entertainment, movies, fine dining have more time for fun! Here are the exact specifications, images, other data on the each from presented in this book the 10 best exotic cars in the completely different from multiple news, media unique presentation. Most of data, images here come from the hundreds of standalone printed and internet sources and confirmed to be true by many exotic car manufacturers.
This sensational book store and always make easy to find all available exact performance and technical specifications for each from best exotic car without days, weeks, months wasted by you on web research and street library research. Those impossible to obtain by car collectors the pictures, important manufacturer car specifications, the design new features descriptions for each exotic car among those rare 10 world best exotic cars are at your fingertips in 1minute inside this Awesome Incredible Book!

10 Best Cars List

You and anybody else could use their own and the very different criteria on creating their own Top10 World Best Cars list. The car experts also do not have the one opinion and one and the same most important criteria to rank all the best fastest, most expensive, exotic cars hand made as the concept cars, prototype cars, limited numbers super small series of cars. One of them are suggesting to rank them by registered top speed. The other would prefer to rank those cars by size of engine or maximum engine power output. Some would even use the specific ratios like amount of the engine maximum horsepower output as ratio to the car weight. Many of them are totally avoiding to even consider official "Manufacturer's Suggested Price of Car" criteria and are dismissing it as not important for the super rich buyers and collectors of the such rare exotic cars. It is true. But author of this book has written it mostly for the regular, ordinary people with big problems to find such money in the millions dollars and pay the manufacturer asked price! The author of this book would use this criteria as his number one and the most important to rank the best modern exotic cars for this updated revised Top10 Best Cars List. The number two, second criteria would be the popularity, world recognition of the rare elite exclusive car Brand Name. Some changes are made to the previous Top10 List from the popular book "Top10 List Fastest Most Expensive Exotic Cars" was published in 2010. The car manufacturers have come up now with the latest and better concept cars and prototype sports cars. "The Earth is not standing still!"

The author could not 100 percent guarantee, that his ranking and this list would remain the same 5-10 years in the near future. In fact nobody could guarantee that everything on presented 10 Best World fastest most expensive rare exotic cars would not change! The car manufacturers are maybe thinking now about building 3-5 years down the road the better prototypes of their sports super cars with the larger, more powerful car engines and the higher car top speeds. Then the author of this book or someone else would offer you their version of the up to date the Top10 Best Cars List!

10 Best Cars List

2012 Bugatti 16.4 Veyron
Price : $2,250,000.00USD
List Rank #1
 See Car Pictures, Specifications on Pages

2006 Ferrari FXX
Price : $1,875,000 USD
List Rank #2
 See Car Pictures, Specifications on Pages

Prices above are Manufacturers Suggested Retail Price
and could be different from auction or dealer prices!

10 Best Cars List

2013 Koenigsegg Agera R
Price : 1,545,568 Euros
List Rank #3
  See Car Pictures, Specifications on Pages

2012 SSC Tuatara
Price : $1,300,000.00USD
List Rank #4
  See Car Pictures, Specifications on Pages

**Prices above are Manufacturers Suggested Retail Price
and could be different from auction or dealer prices!**

10 Best Cars List

1995 McLaren F1 LM
Price : $1,250,000USD
List Rank #5
  See Car Pictures, Specifications on Pages

2009 Pagani Zonda Cinque Roadster
Price : $667,321USD
List Rank #6
  See Car Pictures, Specifications on Pages

Prices above are Manufacturers Suggested Retail Price
and could be different from auction or dealer prices!

Page25

10 Best Cars List

2004 Maserati MC12
Price : $792,000USD
List Rank #7
  See Car Pictures, Specifications on Pages

2012 Lamborghini Avantador J
Price : $557,000USD
List Rank #8
  See Car Pictures, Specifications on Pages

  Prices above are Manufacturers Suggested Retail Price
  and could be different from auction or dealer prices!

10 Best Cars List

2005 LeBlanc Mirabeau
Price : $645,084USD
List Rank #9
 See Car Pictures, Specifications on Pages

2005 Saleen S7 twin turbo
Price : $555,000USD
List Rank #10
 See Car Pictures, Specifications on Pages

Prices above are Manufacturers Suggested Retail Price
and could be different from auction or dealer prices!

2012 Bugatti Veyron 16.4 Grand Sport Vitesse

Art by Stream Information Brokers

General Information

Country of Origin	France
Manufacturer	Bugatti Automobiles S.A.S.
Parent Company	Volkswagen
Chassic Numbers	--
Number of Built cars	3
Years of production	2012
First display at	2012 Geneva Motor Show
Mass Produced Model	2012 Bugatti Veyron 16.4 Grand Sport
Asked Price(MSRP):	$2,250,000.00USD

Prices above are Manufacturers Suggested Retail Price and could be different from auction or dealer prices!

2012 Bugatti Veyron
16.4 Grand Sport Vitesse
New Features in Car Design

The Bugatti had launched a most extreme exotic car built as the Bugatti 16.4 Veyron model in the 2002-2003. But the concept preproduction cars were developed in 1993-1994. The latest and most likely final variation on the Veyron 16.4 concept is the presented here the 2012 Bugatti Veyron 16.4 Grand Sport Vitesse. It is built as the convertible roadster model in difference with the all previous car body versions. The Vitesse (translates from french as "speed") is a mix of the two major existing latest Veyron variations like the Super Sport model with it 1200 horsepower from the quad-turbo 8.0-liter W-16 engine and the targa-topped body of the Grand Sport car version. It is still the one and the only 4400-pound extreme car in difference with the other much more light weight top extreme cars from other exotic car manufacturers. The Vitesse is not just a Grand Sport with the stronger engine and the front and rear fascias of the Super Sport. The driving experience is unique. The Grand Sport Vitesse is the fastest roadster anyone else in the world would drive on the track or open road with an estimated 0-to-60-mph time of 2.4 seconds and a top speed of 255 mph. The air flow turbulence in the open roadster cabin is kept to a minimum because of its relatively small roof opening, carefully engineered airflow around the body shell, and optional wind blocker behind the car seats. Bugatti has tailored a new unique suspension setup for the Vitesse that includes new dampers with faster-working valves and marginally softer springs. This greatly reduced the front-end vibration during full throttle as it is with the Super Sport coupe's steering.

Even at some seriously rash speeds, the Vitesse can be steered with just a couple of fingers on the wheel even on very bumpy roads. The Vitesse is a Veyron Grand Sport convertible with the Super Sport treatment. The made of the alloy engine block for W16 engine is made up of the two exceptionally narrow V8 fit cylinder blocks at an included angle of 90 degrees. In addition to 1200 bhp at 6400 rpm, its 8.0-liter W-16 delivers a highest 1106 lb-ft of torque from 3000 to 5000 rpm as a result of using the same bigger turbos and intercoolers as the Super Sport. The need for more fuel as well as more air to make more power successfully handled with the quad fuel pump setup. The engineers had put more attention to aerodynamic details because the removing the roof changes the way the air flows around the car. The new body design features intended to solve cooling problems and to increase the handling characteristics. The front end airflow, fully paneled undertray with two rear air outlets would greatly reduce the air pressure under the car. The automatically extending rear spoiler increases the down force on the rear wheels and reduces the air resistance at high speeds.
The "smart" rear spoiler, for example, knows whether the detachable hardtop is on or off the car, and so changes its angle of attack to ensure it delivers the same level of the downforce at high speeds (with the roof off, the Vitesse is limited to a mere 233 mph; roof on, it will hit 255 mph). The rear differential oil cooler has been moved from the right-hand side of the car to under the rear diffuser, and the spring rates have been softened slightly to compensate for the reduction in body rigidity. All power from the engine is distributed to all four wheels through a permanent all-wheel drive powertrain. The Haldex 4 wheel drive system funnels more torque to the rear tires in the turns to reduce the car steering problems.

The car is equipped with the Veyron's seven-speed dual disc clutch automated manual transmission developed and built by British engineering company Ricardo. The gear shifts of the new unique seven speed gearbox take place sequentially at paddles behind the steering wheel. The driver operates the transmission without the usual clutch pedal. The double clutch transmission (DCT) shifts from one gear to the next in a maximum of 0.2 of a second. The car has brand new massive 365-710 ZR 540A Michelin car tires. The only thing preventing this Veyron car from going over and beyond the speed of 270 mph is tires. Michelin will only allow two sets of tires (cost about $42,000 a set) to be fitted to the Veyron before the rims, wheels themself (cost $69,000 a set) also have to be replaced to ensure the integrity of the bead seal at high speed. This top extreme Bugatti 16-4 Veyron car rides on new tires developed by Michelin. They are specialty built high speed tires with maximum 400 kmph speed limit, a built-in pressure monitoring system and run-flat 200 kilometers capabilities.

2012 Bugatti Veyron
16.4 Grand Sport Vitesse

Car Performance Specifications

Engine Size   8.0 Liter (487.8 cubic inch)

Engine Power 1200 BHP(896KW)@6400rpm

Engine Torque 1106 ft-lbs(1504Nm)@3000rpm
 Redline RPM   6400rpm

Transmission 7-Speed Automatic w/ Manual Mode
Gearbox   7-speed

Clutch   Twin Disc Clutch

Drive Wheels   All Wheels Drive, AWD

Car Weight   1996 kg (4400 lbs)
Acceleration time 0-60 mph   2.4 sec
Acceleration time 0-60 kmph   2.1 sec.
Acceleration time 0-100 mph: 5.0 sec.
Acceleration time 0-100 kmph: 2.5 sec.
Quarter Mile time and speed: 10.0 sec @146mph
Maximum Skidpad: 1.4 g
Maximum Top Speed: 410kmph (255 mph)
Braking to complete stop , 60-0 mph: 120 ft
Maximum Slalom Speed: 65 mph

Fuel Economy Miles Per Gallon: 8/15mpg(city/hwy)

2012 Bugatti Veyron 16.4 Grand Sport Vitesse

Car Engine Specifications

Manufacturer	Bugatti
Design	72 degrees W16
Location	Mid-engine, Longitudinally
Materials	Aluminum block, heads
Size	8.0 Liter (487.8 cubic inch)
Max. Power	1200 BHP(896KW)@6400rpm
Max. Torque	1106 ft-lbs(1504Nm)@3000rpm
Max. RPM	6400 rpm (redline)
Bore, Stroke	86 mm (3.4 in), 86 mm(3.4 in)
Compression	8.3 : 1
Valvetrain	DOHC, 4valves per cylinder
Fuel	Petrol (Gasoline)
Fuel Delivery	Port fuel injection, quad (4,four) fuel pumps
Aspiration	quad (4,four)-turbochargers
Ignition System	Electronic

2012 Bugatti Veyron
16.4 Grand Sport Vitesse
Car Technical Specifications

Body mfgr   Bugatti Automobiles S.A.S.
Body Design   Coupe Convertible
Body Style   2 Door Targa
Body Materials   Steel, Aluminum
Engine mfgr   Bugatti Automobiles S.A.S.
Engine Size   8.0 Liter (487.8 cubic inch)
Transmission   7-Speed Automatic w/ Manual Mode
Gearbox   7-speed
Clutch   Twin Disc Clutch
Drive Wheels   All Wheels Drive, AWD
Chassis Design   Semi-Monocoque body w/Steel
Front and Rear Subframes,
Chassis Materials Steel, Aluminum
Front Suspension   Coil springs, Shocks, Multi-link,
Control arms, Anti-roll bars
Rear Suspension   Coil springs, Shocks, Multi-link,
Control arms, Anti-roll bars
Car Steering   Rack & Pinion w/Power Assist
Car Front Brakes   Carbon Ceramic Discs
w/Brimbro 8-Piston Calipers
Car Rear Brakes   Carbon Ceramic Discs
w/Brimbro 6-Piston Calipers

2012 Bugatti Veyron 16.4 Grand Sport Vitesse

2012 Bugatti Veyron 16.4 Grand Sport Vitesse

Art by Stream Information Brokers

Overall Car Specifications

Car Length	4463 mm (175.7 in)
Car Width	1999 mm (78.7 in)
Car height	1191 mm (46.9 in)
Car Weight	1996 kg (4400 lbs)
Car wheelbase	2710 mm (106.7 in)
Front wheels track	1715 mm (67.5 in)
Rear wheels track	1618 mm (63.7 in)
Front Wheels	10.5 in x 21 in
Rear Wheels	14.0 in x 21 in
Front Wheel Tires	265-680 ZR 540A Michelin
Rear Wheel Tires	365-710 ZR 540A Michelin

2006 Ferrari FXX

General Information

Country of Origin Italy
Manufacturer   Ferrari S. p. A.
Parent Company   Fiat
Chassic Numbers 145368 -145369
Number of Built cars 30
Years of production 2006-2007
First display at 2005 Bologna Motor Show
Mass Produced Model Ferrari FXX Evoluzione
Asked Price (MSRP): $1,875.000.00USD

**Prices above are Manufacturers Suggested Retail Price
and could be different from auction or dealer prices!**

2006 Ferrari FXX

New Features in Car Design

The design of Ferrari FXX was the successful result of the Ferrari's long term "know how" in building special limited-series sports cars. It had come with the basic framework on which the specifics of future extreme models will be worked out. The Ferrari FXX has similar carbon fibre chassis and greenhouse with mass produced Ferrari Enzo cars. But the front end and rear end were completely redesigned. The revised aerodynamics in new car body design have added the down force increase of 40 percent in total on the front wheels and rear wheels.   The amounts of down force on the rear wheels could be adjusted by the driver with ability to setup the specific angle for the rear spoiler to fit the particular race track. The Ferrari FXX has the redesigned a larger 6.2 liter version of the mass produced by Ferrari 6.0 liter engine found in the Ferrari Enzo and Maserati MC12 exotic sports cars. The new car engine produces at least 800 HP at 8500 rpm.
The redesigned exhausts were re-routed and now exit right under the rear wings, swapping places with the tail lights. The engine -transmission car drive train setup was finished with new similar to Formula 1 car's paddle shifters in order to operate the semiautomatic gearbox that can change gears in less than 100 milliseconds.

The Ferrari FXX has the largest new 19 inch alloy wheels with new specialty designed by tire manufacturer Bridgestone tires in order to have enough space and fit in the extra large Composite Ceramic Material disc brakes with the special brake cooling and pad system specially designed for FXX by famous popular brand name brakes manufacturer Brembo. But the most innovative idea from the Ferrari on this Extreme Exotic Ferrari FXX car is the built into the car the complex telemetry system to monitor and give feedback to a factory trained service technicians on 39 different vehicle dynamics parameters in real time at time of the driving directly from the car on the race track. This system and recorded data would be then analyzed by the Ferrari engineers and designers for next extreme exotic cars design and development!

2006 Ferrari FXX

Car Performance Specifications

Engine Size   6.262Liter(382.1 cubic inch)
Engine Power   800 bhp(597KW)@8500rpm
Engine Torque 509 ft-lbs(690 Nm) @5800rpm
Redline RPM   9000 rpm
Transmission   6-Speed Sequential
Gearbox   6-speed Ferrari F1
Clutch   Twin Disc Clutch
Drive Wheels   Rear Wheels Drive, RWD
Car Weight   1155 kg (2546 lbs)
Acceleration time 0-60 mph   2.9 sec.
Acceleration time 0-60 kmph   2.1 sec.
Acceleration time 0-100 mph   5.2 sec.
Acceleration time 0-100 kmph   3.0 sec.
Quarter Mile time and speed 9.3 sec.@144 mph
Maximum Skidpad   1.05G
Maximum Top Speed   345 kmph(214 mph)
Braking to complete stop , 60-0 mph   109ft
Maximum Slalom Speed   73mph
Fuel Economy Miles Per Gallon: 5/11(city/hwy)

2006 Ferrari FXX

Car Engine Specifications

Manufacturer	Ferrari S. p. A.
Engine Model	Ferrari FXX
Design	65 degree V12
Location	Mid-engine, Longitudinally
Materials	Alloy block and heads
Size	6.262Liter(382.1 cubic inch)
Max. Power	800 bhp(597KW)@8500rpm
Max. Torque	509 ft-lbs(690Nm)@5800rpm
Max. RPM	9000 rpm(redline)
Bore, Stroke	92.0 mm(3.6 in), 78 mm(3.1 in)
Compression	11.6 : 1
Valvetrain	DOHC, 4valves each cylinder
Fuel	Petrol (Gasoline)
Fuel Delivery	Bosch Fuel Injection
Aspiration	Naturally Aspirated
Ignition System	Electronic

2006 Ferrari FXX

Car Technical Specifications

Body mfgr   Ferrari S. p. A.
Body Design   Pininfarina
Body Style   Berlinetta, Coupe
Body Materials   Carbon fiber, Aluminum
Engine mfgr   Ferrari S. p. A.
Engine Size   6.262Liter(382.1 cubic inch)
Transmission   6-Speed Sequential
Gearbox   6-Speed
Clutch   Twin Disc Clutch
Drive Wheels   Rear Wheels Drive, RWD
Chassis Design   Carbon Fiber Body on
Carbon Fiber Monocoque
Chassis Materials Carbon Fiber,Aluminum
Front Suspension   Double wishbones,
Push-rod dampers
Rear Suspension   Double wishbones,
Push-rod dampers
Car Steering   Rack & Pinion
w/Power Assist
Car Front Brakes   Carbon Ceramic Discs,
w/ 6piston Brembo
Car Rear Brakes   Carbon Ceramic Discs,
w/ 4piston Brembo

2006 Ferrari FXX

2006 Ferrari FXX

Overall Car Specifications

Car Length	4702 mm (185.1 in)
Car Width	2035 mm (80.1 in)
Car height	1147 mm (45.2 in)
Car Weight	1155kg (2546.3 lbs)
Car wheelbase	2650 mm (104.3 in)
Front wheels track	1660 mm (65.4 inch)
Rear wheels track	1650 mm (65 inch)
Front Wheels	9.0 in x 19 in
Rear Wheels	13.0 in x 19 in
Front Wheel Tires	245/35 ZR 19 Bridgestone
Rear Wheel Tires	345/35 ZR 19 Bridgestone

2013 Koenigsegg Agera R

General Information

Country of Origin   Sweden
Manufacturer Koenigsegg Automotive AB
Parent Company   -----
Chassic Numbers   -----

Number of Built cars   ---
Years of production   2013
First display at   Auto Show
Mass Produced Model KoenigseggCCX
Asked Price: 1,575,000.00 Euros

Prices above are Manufacturers Suggested Retail Price
and could be different from auction or dealer prices!

2013 Koenigsegg Agera R
New Features in Car Design

The car body has some new features. You would notice at once the redesigned shape of side air intakes and the new headlights. Those changes would provide better cooling for the engine and transmission through increased the intakes' air pressure on the actual cooler and intercooler in order to make them work more efficiently. Car body is also equipped with a front air flow splitter made of carbon fibre material. It is designed to increase the frontal down force from air above on car front wheels and to reduce the air pressure under the car in order to force all car wheels to the ground specially at high speeds. Such design increased the air pressure on the main radiator and brake cooling inlets for the greater performance of this Koenigsegg car. Konigsegg has developed the Twin Fin Wings, a pair of triangular fin-like wings made of carbon fibre to work as the rear spoiler for racing purposes. Their purpose is to increase down force on the rear wheels and to greatly increase the total amount of available power and the torque from engine to be utilized on the car's rear wheels during the high speed driving. The car performance has been improved mainly due to the development of the new more powerful and more lightweight car engine with a new Lysholm supercharger and new titanium exhaust. These components help engine' power reach the maximum limit at 806 HP or 1018 HP, while maintaining a torque in wide range of low to high engine' rpm (rotation speed in revolutions per minute). The new Koenigsegg Agera super car runs on the biofuel like the 2007-2010 CCXR cars. But the car's engine also functions with an E85 green fuel.

The fuel system of the Agera R has been upgraded to give the future users the chance to experience 1140 horsepower and a maximum torque of 885 lb-ft on E85 or E100 biofuel. The Koenigsegg car's owners can also opt out for the normal petrol (gasoline) use due to the car's flexfuel system.

The Koenigsegg car engine is equipped with a new Lysholm Screw Compressor with several advantages to the common centrifugal compressor. It would create a higher boost-pressure at lower rpm to increase both acceleration and control at low speed. Lag time during shifts and on-off throttling is reduced to a minimum. The new twin screw design is also highly energy efficient to deliver the extreme power and torque of this car. The Koenigsegg's team of engineers has implemented Formula One car racing technology in the construction of the new Koenigsegg CCR Cylindrical Throttle. It is a vital part of their effort to optimize the intake air flow to the engine and reduce the air resistance or drag to a minimum. The new Koenigsegg CCXR engine incorporates a new unique air intake plenum chamber made of carbon fibre. It was designed and modeled by the Koenigsegg company engineers exclusively for the CCR. It helps to increase the engine's performance in a number of ways. It lowers the weight of the car by around 11 kg. It provides a more aerodynamic flow of air into the engine and moves the pressure center closer to cylinders with reduction in the throttle lag time. The intake plenum is shaped to allow a stream of cooling air pass between it and the engine block in order to keep the charged intake air as cool as possible. The CCR has made from titanium the complete exhaust system. It brings several advantages to this record-braking supercar. The exhaust system could be more lightweight with the same strength as while built from steel but virtually insensitive to high temperature.

Using this extraordinary metal enables the construction of an exhaust system out of very thin material without adding extra heat insulation, which adds to the efficiency of the catalytic converters. The CCR Titanium Exhaust system weighs less than half of its stainless steel predecessor without need for extra heat insulation. It is also slightly refined in the design of the manifolds in order to further minimize drag. The Koenigsegg CCR brakes are specially developed for the model by AP-Racing. They feature a new technology that ensures perfectly intact braking ability regardless of the unavoidable thermal shifts in the brake-disc. The discs are not mounted in a fixed position to the wheels, but are allowed to move a fraction of a millimeter in all directions, that describe as floating mount. This serves to absorb any thermal shift, which in combination with the Koenigsegg brake ventilation system makes the brakes exceptionally stable at any driving (racing) condition. Koenigsegg has chosen the steel alloy for brake discs. The CCR is equipped with new shock absorbers, custom built and developed for the Koenigsegg CCR by VPS, Italy. These superb shocks have smaller weight and allow extensive fine tuning to suit the racetrack or driver preferences. The Agera R comes with a super light carbon fiber wheel that allows drivers to enjoy and stay safe in the car. This new technology developed by Koenigsegg is called the Aircore Technology. It saves up to 44 pounds of the unsprung mass and makes sure that the driving system is safe and precise. The wheel of the Agera car works in the tandem with Koenigsegg Electronic Stability which can be found on every single Koenigsegg car.

2013 Koenigsegg Agera R
Car Performance Specifications

Engine Size   5.0Liter (305.1 Cubic inch)
Engine Power   1140 HP(850KW)@7100rpm
Engine Torque   885 ft-lbs(1203Nm)@4100rpm
Redline RPM   7500 rpm
Transmission   Cima 7-Speed Manual AP
Gearbox   7-speed manual
Clutch   Twin Disc Clutch
Drive Wheels   Rear Wheels Drive, RWD
w/ Electronic Differential
Car Weight   1435 kg (3163 lbs)
Acceleration time 0-60 mph   2.8 sec.
Acceleration time 0-60 kmph   2.3 sec
Acceleration time 0-100 mph: 7.9 sec
Acceleration time 0-100 kmph: 2.9 sec.
Quarter Mile time and speed: 9.0 sec@146mph
Maximum Skidpad: 1.60g
Maximum Top Speed: 442kmph (273 mph)
Braking to complete stop , 60-0 mph: 110 ft
Maximum Slalom Speed: 67 mph
Fuel Economy Miles Per Gallon: 10/15 mpg(city/hwy)

2013 Koenigsegg Agera R

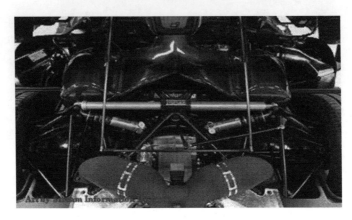

Car Engine Specifications

Manufacturer	Koenigsegg Automotive AB
Design	V8
Location	Mid-Engine, Longitudinally
Materials	Alluminum Block, Head
Size	5.0Liter (305.1 Cubic inch)
Max. Power	1140 HP(850KW)@7100rpm
Max. Torque	885 ft-lbs(1203 Nm)@4100rpm
Max. RPM	7500 rpm(redline)
Bore, Stroke	91 mm(3.6 in), 95.25mm(3.75 in)
Compression	9.0:1
Valvetrain	DOHC, 4 Valves per Cylinder
Fuel	Bio Fuel , E85, Petrol(gasoline)
Fuel Delivery	Multi-Point Fuel Injection
Aspiration	Twin Superchargers
Ignition System	Electronic Coil on Plug

2013 Koenigsegg Agera R
Car Technical Specifications

Body mfgr   Koenigsegg Automotive AB

Body Design   Semi-Monocoque

Body Style   2 Door Coupe

Body Materials Carbon Fiber, Aluminum,

Engine mfgr   Koenigsegg Automotive AB

Engine Size   5.0Liter(305.1 Cubic inch)

Transmission   Cima 7-Speed Manual

Gearbox   7-speed manual

Clutch   Twin Disc Clutch

Drive Wheels   Rear Wheels Drive, RWD
w/Torque Sensitive Limited Slip
Differential

Chassis Design   Aluminum Honeycomb,
Subframes, Hydraulic
Lifting system

Chassis Materials Carbon Fibre, Aluminum

Front Suspension   Double Wishbones w/Pushrod
Operated Upsl Adjustable Gas
Shock Absorbers

Rear Suspension   Double Wishbones w/Pushrod
Operated Upsl Adjustable Gas
Shock Absorbers, Triplex Damper

Car Steering   Rack & Pinion w/Power Assist

Car Front Brakes   Carbon Ceramic Discs
w/Brimbro 6-Piston Calipers

Car Rear Brakes   Carbon Ceramic Discs
w/Brimbro 4-Piston Calipers

2013 Koenigsegg AgeraR

2013 Koenigsegg AgeraR

Overall Car Specifications

Car Length	4293 mm(169.0 inch)
Car Width	1996 mm(78.6 inch)
Car height	1120 mm(44.1 inch)
Car Weight	1435 kg (3163 lbs)
Car wheelbase	2662 mm (104.8 in)
Front wheels track	1700 mm (66.9 in)
Rear wheels track	1650 mm (65 in)
Front Wheels	9.5 in x 19 in
Rear Wheels	12.5 in x 20 in
Front Wheel Tires	265/35 - 19 Michelin
Rear Wheel Tires	345/30 - 20 Michelin

2012 SSC Tuatara

General Information

Country of Origin   USA
Manufacturer   Shelby Supercars
Parent Company   SSC North America
Chassic Numbers   --
Number of Built cars   7
Years of production   2012
First display at   2011 Dubai Motor Show
Mass Produced Model 2013 SSC Ultimate
Aero XT
Asked Price: $1,300,000.00USD

Prices above are Manufacturers Suggested Retail Price
and could be different from auction or dealer prices!

Page55

2012 SSC Tuatara
New Features in Car Design

The SSC North America company also formerly known as the Shelby Supercars Inc. has unveiled their new creation and the 1350HP RWD beast 2011-2012 SSC Tuatara racing sports super car! The engineers and the designers have made everything to overcome the dreaded forces of nature at 200+ mph while packaging the required mechanical components. It is the ultimate example of the form meeting function, to create a harmonious whole thing. Everybody like the black teardrop-shaped canopy that sits on top of the white exterior, creating a stunning contrast of power and beauty. The shape is classic and pivotal, and has a very low drag coefficient. The car features dihedral stabilizers or wings that have been borrowed from the realm of aviation. The new term "flying buttress" might be construed as a being a bit naughty, but they are actuallythe wings that help support the structure of the car. In this case, they are those bits on the side of the SSC Tuatara to channel air toward the engine intakes. The front of the car looks intimidating and purposeful with its low slung nose and carbon fiber headlights. Looking closely, you'll notice venting for the carbon brakes and a cohesive front splitter that generates enough down force to keep the nose planted at speed. There is no hood or luggage space, or any kind of compromise with this car. The side profile is sleek and sexy.   There are no door handles or side repeaters and the car barely stands over a meter tall. Massive lower recesses house air intakes in front of the rear wheel arches and feed the ravenous engine and cooling radiators with much-needed cold air, while doing its bit to balance the look. It checks all the hyper car boxes and then some more. Elements of the first Aero are maintained, most notably the party piece doors and simple-spoked wheel design.

The entire body and the chassis, save for the front and rear impact zones, are all made from the carbon fiber - further emphasizing lightness as key. This is not necessarily for top speed, but more for everyday driving and handling.

All mid-engine cars require the apertures in the bodywork to help get rid of heat – they usually take the form of slats or louvers but since this car is anything but, it features circular cut outs in various diameters to expel heat and generate the public's controversy. Moving to the other worldly rear, the dynamics take over, with the aesthetics playing second fiddle. The entire under a floor of the car is sealed leading up to the rear which functions as the mother of all diffusers, complete with the F1-style exhaust.   This one record breaker car is powered by a quad-cam, twin-turbo V8 displacing 6.8 liters. The engine and all the other mechanical parts for this car were all designed and developed in-house by the SSC own engineers and designers. This new powerplant shares a lot with the old 6.2 liter item – the block and its innards are the same design, so are the dimensions and location of its all 10 radiators.   Changes come in the form of a four valves per cylinder overhead cam (OHC) setup as opposed to the well-known usual push rods valves' open-close setup.

The changes continues with the new SSC spec turbochargers. The new setup is good for a colossal 1350 bhp at 9000rpm! Zero to 62mph will arrive in around 2.8 seconds and SSC claims a top speed of the 275mph!   The in gear acceleration figures are not known as of yet, but you can be sure they will be absolutely mind blowing.   Thank goodness the new car will feature all four wheels traction control, anti-lock brakes ABS with the servo assistance, and the Brembo carbon ceramic brakes.   This SSC Tuatara super car has only the RWD drivetrain. The engineers made this way the car much lighter than 4wd or AWD supercars by other manufacturers.

Page57

Its weight is just under 1200kg. The SSC engineers were surprised with the shown registered time for the tested SSC Tuatara car to reach 200 mph. They has figured out and determined the perfect gear ratios for the brand new 7-speed Tuatara transmission. The latter being the first ever one piece carbon fiber wheels ever fitted to a car. They are the products of the Australian company named Carbon Revolution. The 19" front wheels weigh just 5.8kg each. There is a hydraulically operated air brake between the rear stabilizers. It comes into play at higher-than-allowed speeds. The SSC Tuatara is slightly more narrow than before to comply with the FIA GT regulations, should they decide to race it. This futuristic interior was developed following aerospace design found on the exterior. In fact, many of the interior elements found on the Tuatara resemble specific elements of the exterior. For example, the two small, informational HUD displays situated on the left and right of the driver are all inspired by the Tuatara's rear winglets and the central AC vents were inspired by the Tuatara's twin central exhausts. The holes pattern on the top of the central console area are inspired by the hole patterns on the Tuatara's exterior body panels and the door pulls even have their exterior counterpart in the interior from the rear sides of the car. The previously mentioned HUD displays are joined by a main gauge cluster area that is in fact a glass screen is lit up by Pico projectors and is similar to a HUD (Heads Up Display). The right HUD will offer information on the current gear of the car, while the left HUD will let the driver choose the info he needs using a menu on the central command console. But the dedication to every small detail doesn't stop at excellent performance. The special race-ready seats are designed to accommodate a tall driver up to 6'7" height and 300 lbs weight.

Page58

Standard features include power windows, power locks, security system, the DVD player, a backup camera, height adjustment, premium sounds system, five-light sequential shift indicator and a horsepower gauge. A "Start" button will initiate a clockwise-motion lighting sequence on the red lights located around the start button. When all these lights turn on the engine will start. The central console features buttons located near the touch screen and help the driver to control functions like traction control, driving modes, etc. Even the front passenger can stay well-informed in the Tuatara as SSC has included two small screens that provide him details on the current speed, RPM, or BHP. One of the best features of the interior, however, is the seven-speed H-pattern manual gear shift designed after classic exotics. An automatic unit will also be offered in a steering column mounted seven-speed paddle shifter.

2012 SSC Tuatara
Car Performance Specifications

Engine Size   6.867Liter(423.6 Cubic inch)

Engine Power   1350BHP(759KW)@9000rpm

Engine Torque 1042 ft-lbs(1417Nm)@6800rpm

Redline RPM   9200

Transmission   7-speed SMG paddle shifter

Gearbox   7-speed manual

Clutch   Triple Disc Clutch

Drive Wheels   Rear Wheels Drive, RWD

Car Weight   1248 kg (2750 lbs)

Acceleration time 0-60 mph   2.5 sec.

Acceleration time 0-60 kmph   2.1 sec.

Acceleration time 0-100 mph   8.2 sec.

 Acceleration time 0-100 kmph   2.4 sec.

Quarter Mile time and speed   9.6 sec. @144mph

Maximum Skidpad   1.45g

Maximum Top Speed: 455 kmph (276mph)

Braking to complete stop , 60-0 mph: 103fts

Maximum Slalom Speed   72 mph

Fuel Economy Miles Per Gallon 7/12 (city/hwy)

2012 SSC Tuatara

Car Engine Specifications

Manufacturer	SSC North America
Design	V8
Location	Mid-Engine, Longitudinally
Materials	Aluminum Block, Heads
Size	6.876Liter (423.6 Cubic inch)
Max. Power	1350BHP(759KW)@9000rpm
Max. Torque	1042 ft-lbs(1417Nm)@6800rpm
Max. RPM	9200 rpm(redline)
Bore, Stroke	104.8 mm(4.1 in), 92 mm(3.62 in)
Compression	8.625 :1
Valvetrain	Quad (4,four) Camshafts setup, OHC , 4 valves per Cylinder
Fuel	Petrol (Gasoline)
Fuel Delivery	Electronic Sequential Multi Port Injection
Aspiration	Twin Turbos
Ignition System	Electronic

2012 SSC Tuatara

Car Technical Specifications

Body mfgr	SSC North America
Body Design	Semi-Monocoque
Body Style	2 Door Coupe
Body Materials	Carbon fiber, Aluminum
Engine mfgr	SSC North America
Engine Size	6.876Liter(423.6Cubic inch)
Transmission	7-Speed Manual AP
Gearbox	7-speed manual
Clutch	Triple Disc Clutch
Drive Wheels	Rear Wheels Drive, RWD
Chassis Design	Semi-Monocoque body w/Steel Front and Rear Aluminum Subframes, Air Lifting system
Chassis Materials	Carbon Fibre, Aluminum
Front Suspension	Unequal Length Upper and Lower A-Arms, Coils over Adjustable Shock Absorbers, Anti-roll Bar
Rear Suspension	Unequal Length Upper and Lower A-Arms, Coils over Adjustable Shock Absorbers, Anti-roll Bar
Car Steering	Rack & Pinion w/ Electric Assist
Car Front Brakes	Carbon Ceramic Discs w/ 8-Piston Calipers
Car Rear Brakes	Carbon Ceramic Discs w/ 6-Piston Calipers

2012 SSC Tuatara

2012 SSC Tuatara

Overall Car Specifications

Car Length	4430 mm (174.4 inch)
Car Width	1991 mm (78.4 inch)
Car height	1092 mm (43 inch)
Car Weight	1248 kg (2750 lbs)
Car wheelbase	2667 mm (105 inch)
Front wheels track	1750 mm (68.9 in)
Rear wheels track	1650 mm (65.0 in)
Front Wheels	19 in x 9-1/2 in, Carbon Fiber
Rear Wheels	20 in x 13 in, Carbon Fiber
Front Wheel Tires	235 35 (YR)19 Michelin PS2
Rear Wheel Tires	335 30 (YR)20 Michelin PS2

1995 McLaren F1 LM

General Information

Country of Origin	Great Britain
Manufacturer	McLaren Cars Ltd
Parent Company	------
Chassic Numbers	XP1 LM
Number of Built cars	6
Years of production	1994-1995
First display at	Auto Show
Mass Produced Model	McLaren F1 GTR
Asked Price	$1,250,000.00USD

Prices above are Manufacturers Suggested Retail Price
and could be different from auction or dealer prices!

1995 McLaren F1 LM
New Features in Car Design

The McLaren had launched it Best Top exotic supercar development only after long preparations. The car chassis XP1 LM was the prototype that formed the basis for the five production cars McLaren F1 LMs, that were built to celebrate McLaren's victory in the 24 Hours of Le Mans. To ensure that there was plenty of performance, the designer made the car as light as possible. The engine power would easy overcome the weight in a straight line. But during the braking and the cornering every kilogram counted. This was achieved by using a host of the exotic and composite materials, with the carbon fibre the most prominent. The car body designers used many banned by that time in the Formula 1 cars design the ground effects and moving aerodynamics for the design of this McLaren F1 LM sports road car. It includes big rear spoiler-wing. The McLaren F1 LM car was fitted with the two electric fans to suck the car to the ground. Car also has a small moveable wing on the tail of the car that offered the stability at high speed, served as an airbrake and as additional cooling vent for the rear brakes. These large aerodynamic improvements provided plenty of the down force, but without the drag created by the familiar big wings.

The car designers from McLaren decided to use the already manufactured by BMW car engine in order to speed up the design of car process. The manufacturer BMW not only met the requirements by McLaren. The 6.1 liter, 627 bhp V12 engine for the McLaren GTR racing version exceeded the 550 bhp set, although it was slightly heavier than asked for. McLaren used a restrictor-free version of the GTR engine for this new McLaren F1 LM road car. Stripped from the restrictor plates engine produced a staggering 680 bhp.

The lightweight V12 engine was mounted amidships and mated to the McLaren-developed six speed manual gearbox. To better insulate the heat from the tight engine bay, the engine and exhaust covers were covered in gold, which is highly reflective to the heat.

The supercars are "no compromise" driving machines with the performance as the main focus with the little or need at all for practicality and comfort. The interior also featured a

highly advanced cd-player, but no radio. Ahead of both rear wheels there were two storage bins that could take as much luggage as a small hatchback of the day. To provide the driver with a genuine direct feel and again to save weight, advanced driving aids like a 'flappy-paddle gearbox'.

The car was not equipped with the ABS brakes, the power steering and wheels' traction control .

1995 McLaren F1 LM

Car Performance Specifications

Engine Size	6.06Liter(370 Cubic inch)
Engine Power	680BHP(507KW)@7800rpm
Engine Torque	520 ft-lbs(705Nm)@4500rpm
Redline RPM	8500 rpm
Transmission	6-Speed Manual w/AP
Gearbox	6-speed manual
Clutch	Triple-Plate Clutch
Drive Wheels	Rear Wheels Drive, RWD
Car Weight	1062 kg (2341.3 lbs)
Acceleration time 0-60 mph	3.5 sec.
Acceleration time 0-60 kmph	2.5 sec.
Acceleration time 0-100 mph	6.7 sec.
Acceleration time 0-100 kmph	3.8 sec.
Quarter Mile time and speed	11.0 sec.@130mph
Maximum Skidpad	0.94g
Maximum Top Speed	365kmph (225mph)
Braking to complete stop , 60-0 mph	127 ft
Maximum Slalom Speed	64.5 mph
Fuel Economy Miles Per Gallon	6/12(city/hwy)

1995 McLaren F1 LM

Car Engine Specifications

Manufacturer	BMW
Model	S70/2 GTR
Design	60degrees V12
Location	Mid-engine, Longitudinally
Materials	Alloy block and head
Size	6.064 Liter (370 cubic inch)
Max. Power	680BHP(507KW)@7800rpm
Max. Torque	520 ft-lbs(705Nm)@4500rpm
Max. RPM	8500 rpm(redline)
Bore, Stroke	86mm(3.39 in), 87mm (3.43 in)
Compression	11 : 1
Valvetrain	DOHC, 4valves each cylinder
Fuel	Petrol (Gasoline)
Fuel Delivery	Fuel Injection
Aspiration	Naturally Aspirated
Ignition System	Electronic

1995 McLaren F1 LM

Car Technical Specifications

Body mfgr	McLaren Cars Ltd
Body Design	Monocoque
Body Style	2 Door Coupe
Body Materials	Carbon fiber, Aluminum
Engine mfgr	BMW
Engine Size	6.064Liter (370 Cubic inch)
Transmission	6-Speed Manual w/AP
Gearbox	6-speed manual
Clutch	Twin Disc Clutch
Drive Wheels	Rear Wheels Drive, RWD w/Torsen Differential
Chassis Design	Monocoque body with Subframe
Chassis Materials	Carbon Fibre, Aluminum
Front Suspension	Double Wishbones, Alloy Dampers, Co-Axial Coil Springs
Rear Suspension	Double Wishbones, Alloy Dampers, Co-Axial Coil Springs
Car Steering	Unassisted Rack & Pinion
Car Front Brakes	Unassisted Vented & Crossdrilled Discs
Car Rear Brakes	Unassisted Vented & Crossdrilled Discs

1995 McLaren F1 LM

1995 McLaren F1 LM

Art by Stream Information Brokers

Overall Car Specifications

Car Length	4365 mm (171.9 in)
Car Width	1920 mm (75.6 in)
Car height	1120 mm (44.1 in)
Car Weight	1062kg (2341.3 lbs)
Car wheelbase	2718 mm (107.0 in)
Front wheels track	1570 mm (61.8 in)
Rear wheels track	1464 mm (57.6 in)
Front Wheels	10.5 in x 18 in
Rear Wheels	13.5 in x 18 in
Front Wheel Tires	275/35 ZR 18
Rear Wheel Tires	345/35 ZR 18

2009 Pagani Zonda Cinque Roadster

Art by Stream Information Brokers

General Information

Country of Origin	Italy
Manufacturer	Pagani Automobili S.p.A.
Parent Company	----
Chassic Numbers	76104
Number of Built cars	5
Years of production	2008-2009
First display at	2008 Geneva Motor Show
Mass Produced Model	2013 Pagani Huayra
Asked Price:	$2,535,000.00US

Prices above are Manufacturers Suggested Retail Price
and could be different from auction or dealer prices!

2009 Pagani Zonda Cinque Roadster

New Features in Car Design

This really exotic fastest and expensive street legal super car produced only in 5 (five) limited pieces. It was the first Pagani car equipped with a sequential gearbox manageable both with paddles behind the steering wheel and with the traditional gear shifter on the central floor tunnel. It was the first Zonda car to use the new Pagani invention. Brand new carbon-titanium material was used to produce the car body and chassis. It is the special fiber purposely created for the Zonda Cinque car. This new lightweight and strong material will be eventually used on the new generation models.

All weight reduction measures adopted by Pagani to improve the driving pleasure, the car performance and the engine's emission of the Zonda Cinque have found use in the Cinque Roadster as well. The Carbon-Titanium chassis has been redesigned for the compensation of a missing roof.

The Cinque experience is enhanced with the roof stored in the front bonnet, when the storm of the air being fed to the 678hp Mercedes AMG V12 engine through the massive intake just inches over the passengers' ears, accompanied by the exhaust note of the bespoke Zonda Cinque Inconel and Titanium exhaust system. The car body is equipped with a longer front spoiler, a new designed rear wing, a central air intake on monocoque, extra air intakes for rear brakes.

The unique aerodynamic features like the flat car body bottom and new rear air extractors had improved the down force up to 750 Kg at 300km. This super car has the 678 bhp maximum power from engine, the maximum 780 Nm torque, forged monolock titanium wheels, bolts and nuts are done in titanium and boast the Pagani logo. The suspension and springs made with the titanium developed with the latest technology and in accordance with the Pagani specifications. This unique suspension has the four different settings, the 10 adjustments each, to separate high and low frequencies, both in compression and extension suspension work cycles. The interiors are refined and at the same time reveal the sporting attitude of this car. The racing leather seats were developed by Toora. The car is equipped with the safety 4-points car racing seatbelts and molybdenum steel rollover passengers protection bars with carbon fiber coating.

The Zonda Cinque roadster has the brand new specialty designed Pirelli tires, with special compounds for this car.

.

2009 Pagani Zonda Cinque Roadster

Car Performance Specifications

Engine Size	7.291Liter(444 Cubic inch)
Engine Power	678BHP(506KW)@6150rpm
Engine Torque	575ft-lbs(780Nm)@4000 rpm
Redline RPM	6300rpm
Transmission	6-Speed Semi-automatic
Gearbox	6-speed manual
Clutch	Twin Disc Clutch
Drive Wheels	Rear Wheels Drive, RWD
Car Weight	1210 kg (2667 lbs)
Acceleration time 0-60 mph	3.3 sec.
Acceleration time 0-60 kmph	3.2 sec.
Acceleration time 0-100 mph	9.4 sec.
Acceleration time 0-100 kmph	9.1 sec.
Quarter Mile time and speed	11.1 sec.@127 mph
Maximum Skidpad	1.45G
Maximum Top Speed	350kmph (217 mph)
Braking to complete stop , 60-0 mph	116 ft
Maximum Slalom Speed	69.3 mph
Fuel Economy Miles Per Gallon	8/13 (city/hwy)

2006Pagani Zonda
Cinque Roadster

Car Engine Specifications

Manufacturer	Daimler-Benz
Make, Model	Mercedes-AMG M120
Design	60 degree V12
Location	Mid-engine, Longitudinally
Materials	Aluminum block, heads
Size	7.291Liter(444Cubic inch)
Max. Power	678BHP(506KW)@6150rpm
Max. Torque	575 ft-lbs(780 Nm)@4000rpm
Max. RPM	6500 rpm (redline)
Bore, Stroke	91.5mm(3.6 in), 92.4mm(3.6 in)
Compression	9.2:1
Valvetrain	DOHC, 4valves per Cylinder
Fuel	Petrol (Gasoline)
Fuel Delivery	Fuel Injection
Aspiration	Naturally Aspirated
Ignition System	Electronic

2009 Pagani Zonda Cinque Roadster

Car Technical Specifications

Body mfgr	Pagani Automobili S.p.A.
Body Design	Central Monocoque
Body Style	2 Door Roadster
Body Materials	Carbon fiber, Titanium
Engine mfgr	Daimler-Benz
Engine Size	7.291Liter(444Cubic inch)
Transmission	6-Speed Sequential
Gearbox	6-speed manual
Clutch	Twin Disc Clutch
Drive Wheels	Rear Wheels Drive, RWD
Chassis Design	Central Monocoque
Chassis Materials	Carbon Fibre,Aluminum
Front Suspension	Double Wishbones w/Pushrod activated Coil Springs, adjustable Shock Absorbers, Anti-Roll Bar
Rear Suspension	Double Wishbones w/Pushrod activated Coil Springs, adjustable Shock Absorbers, Anti-Roll Bar
Car Steering	Rack & Pinion w/Power Assist
Car Front Brakes	Ceramic Discs, 6 -piston Brembo
Car Rear Brakes	Ceramic Discs , 4-piston Brembo

2009 Pagani Zonda Cinque Roadster

2009 Pagani Zonda
Cinque Roadster

Art by Stream Information Brokers

Overall Car Specifications

Car Length	4435 mm (174.6 inch)
Car Width	2055 mm (80.9 inch)
Car height	1141 mm (44.9 inch)
Car Weight	1210 kg (2667 lbs)
Car wheelbase	2730 mm (107.5 inch)
Front wheels track	1800 mm (70.9 in)
Rear wheels track	1720 mm (67.7 in)
Front Wheels	19.0 in x 9.0 in
Rear Wheels	20.0 in x 12.5 in
Front Wheel Tires	255/35/19 Pirelli
Rear Wheel Tires	335/30/20 Pirelli

2004 Maserati MC12

General Information

Country of Origin	Italy
Manufacturer	Maserati
Parent Company	------
Chassic Numbers	--
Number of Built cars	50
Years of production	2004-2005
First display at	2004 Geneva Motor Show
Mass Produced Model	Maserati MC12 GTR
Asked Price:	$792,000.00USD

Prices above are Manufacturers Suggested Retail Price
and could be different from auction or dealer prices!

2004Maserati MC12
New Features in Car Design

This extreme sports Maserati MC12 car got the functional styling focused toward the better aerodynamics. The air intakes, vents and other aerodynamic components have been designed to optimize the car's internal fluid aerodynamics and air flows to ensure optimal down force (a vertical load) and the aerodynamic efficiency values. The channels along the each side of the car stretches from the front wheel vent to an inlet just in front of the rear wheel. This solution contributes to aerodynamic down force while also improving the car's body aerodynamic efficiency. There is a snorkel with the air intake for the engine compartment just above the hard top. The car body has the rear two-meter carbon wing with the two fins and a small spoiler at its base with the third stop light installed. The inverted half moon design of the exhausts is the most striking part of the tail section. The whole under the car chassic has been faired in and sealed and there are the two generous diffusers that also delivered the maximum "ground effect" noise. The MC12 car engine carried on all of the Ferrari Maserati Group's most advanced technologies and the competition experience. The car is powered by an impressive Ferrari made 630 hp six-liter mid-car V12 engine and boasts 41%-front and 59%-rear weight distribution. This powerful Naturally Aspirated 12-cylinder 65E V engine displaces the 5998 cc and punches out 638BHP or 465 kW at the 7500 rpm.

It had been being designed to meet the specific needs and the characteristics of a road-going Maserati with the excellent awesome drivability. The MC12 delivers a maximum torque of the 652 Nm at 5500 rpm and remains exceptionally nimble and fluid even at low engine speeds. It has an aluminum alloy made crankcase, the titanium made con rods, and extremely aerodynamically efficient four-valve cylinder heads to boot. The valves timing executed by the work of the four overhead gear-driven camshafts per cylinder with the perfect control. The dry sump lubrication also boasts a highly efficient scavenger pump. The MC12's performance-oriented engine design ha d fitted perfectly with the six-speed Maserati own Cambiocorsa transmission with offering the computerized gear selection. The driver doesn't need to touch the clutch with this electro-hydraulic controlled gearbox and instead selects the gears using the paddles mounted behind the steering wheel. The transmission's two modes are selected at the touch of a button. The Sport mode will be the driver's most frequent choice and include a good dose of the active traction control, while the Race setting enhances the kind of sporty behavior typically seen on the track. In the Race mode the system delivers much nippier gear changing and also activates the ASR. The lightweight Maserati MC12 car is a two-seater long-tail coupe-spider with a quite long wheel base (2800 mm). It has a typical racing/sporty set-up with a removable hard top. Highly advanced composites and alloys have enhanced its structural rigidity and kept its overall weight down.

The MC12 car's bodywork is entirely made from the carbon fibre. And its stress-bearing chassis is made from a carbon fibre and Nomex honeycomb sandwich. The two made from the aluminum sub-frames in the chassis's design support the ancillaries, helps absorb bumps, and guarantee an excellent standard of safety. The cabin boasts an easily removable top, which instantly converts the MC12 from a coupe to a spider. The cabin itself is the epitome of the best elegance and sport, race car attributes. The instruments are organized around a central and prominent speedometer and placed directly in front of the driver. The center console includes the controls for the climate control system and two of its four vents. Set at the intersection of the console and the central tunnel is the characteristic oval clock, and the blue engine Start button. Other controls are laid out on the titanium-colored stylized central tunnel which also includes a storage compartment and a 12-volt outlet. The seats have a carbon fibre structure with high lateral containment. The seats themselves are upholstered in fabric with the shoulder rests in perforated leather. The doors have the carbon fibre interior panels and pockets complete with the electric window operation buttons. The pedals are aluminum and the mats made from rubber.

2004 Maserati MC12
Car Performance Specifications

Engine Size   6.0Liter(366 cubic inch)

Engine Power   630BHP(470KW)@7500rpm

Engine Torque   481ft-lbs(652 Nm)@5500 rpm

Redline RPM   7800 rpm

Transmission   6 speed Semi-automatic

Gearbox   6-speed Ferrari F1

Clutch   Twin Disc Clutch

Drive Wheels   Rear Wheels Drive, RWD

Car Weight   1335 kg (2943.2 lbs)

Acceleration time 0-60 mph   3.4 sec.

Acceleration time 0-60 kmph   2.1 sec.

Acceleration time 0-100 mph   7.1 sec.

Acceleration time 0-100 kmph   3.5 sec.

Quarter Mile time and speed 11.3 sec.@131 mph

Maximum Skidpad   0.93g

Maximum Top Speed   330kmph (205 mph)

Braking to complete stop , 60-0 mph   108 ft

Maximum Slalom Speed   69.8 mph

Fuel Economy Miles Per Gallon 6/10 (city/hwy)

2004 Maserati MC12

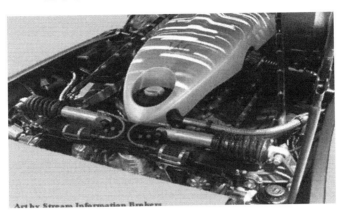

Art by Stream Information Brokers

Car Engine Specifications

Manufacturer	Ferrari
Model	Tipo F140B
Design	V12
Location	Mid-engine, Longitudinally
Materials	Aluminum block, heads
Size	6.0 Liter (366 cubic inch)
Max. Power	630BHP(470KW)@7500rpm
Max. Torque	481ft-lbs(652 Nm)@5500rpm
Max. RPM	7800 rpm (redline)
Bore, Stroke	92.0mm(3.6 inch),75.2mm(3.0 inch)
Compression	11.2 : 1
Valvetrain	DOHC, 4 valves per cylinder, VVT
Fuel	Petrol (Gasoline)
Fuel Delivery	Bosch Fuel Injection
Aspiration	Naturally Aspirated
Ignition System	Bosch Electronic

2004 Maserati MC12
Car Technical Specifications

Body mfgr	Maserati
Body Design	Maserati Centro Stile
Body Style	2 Door Coupe
Body Materials	Carbon fiber
Engine mfgr	Ferrari
Engine Size	6.0Liter (366 Cubic inch)
Transmission	6-Speed Semiautomatic
Gearbox	6-speed
Clutch	Twin Disc Clutch
Drive Wheels	Rear Wheels Drive, RWD
Chassis Design	Honeycomb Monocoque body with Front and Rear Aluminum Subframes,
Chassis Materials	Carbon Fibre, Aluminum
Front Suspension	Double Wishbones w/Pushrod operated coil springs over dampers
Rear Suspension	Double Wishbones w/Pushrod operated coil springs over dampers
Car Steering	Rack & Pinion w/Power Assist
Car Front Brakes	ABS vented Disks
Car Rear Brakes	ABS vented Discs

2004 Maserati MC12

2004 Maserati MC12

Overall Car Specifications

Car Length	5143 mm (202.5 in)
Car Width	2096 mm (82.5 in)
Car height	1205 mm (47.4 in)
Car Weight	1335 kg (2943.2 lbs)
Car wheelbase	2800 mm (110.2 in)
Front wheels track	1660 mm (65.4 in)
Rear wheels track	1660 mm (65.4 in)
Front Wheels	245/35/19 in
Rear Wheels	345/35/19 in
Front Wheel Tires	245/35 ZR 19

2012 Lamborghini Aventador J

General Information

Country of Origin   Italy

Manufacturer Automobili Lamborghini   S. p. A.

Parent Company   ----

Chassic Numbers   ----

Number of Built cars   4

Years of production   2012

First display at 2012 Geneva Motor Show

Mass Produced Model   Lamborghini
Sesto Elemento

Asked Price: 1,500,000.00Euros

Prices above are Manufacturers Suggested Retail Price
and could be different from auction or dealer prices!

2012 Lamborghini Aventador J

New Features in Car Design

The Aventador J offers its pilot and copilot the exclusive experience of the power and dynamics. At the same time, the 515 kW / 700 hp two-seater is a first class the technology showcase, combining innovative solutions and brand-new materials and demonstrating the Automobili Lamborghini's enormous expertise in the carbon fiber technology. This car is a radically open automobile. The exterior and interior are meld into each other. The designers and engineers from the Sant'Agata Bolognese have not only dispensed entirely with the roof, but also with the front windshield. This requires that drivers of the Aventador J must have the right equipment for driving at top speeds higher than 300 kmph. This car the Lamborghini Aventador J is fully functional for road use. It is also an absolute one-of-a-kind piece of art. The car prototype for the Aventador J is the Aventador LP 700-4 - Lamborghini's new twelve-cylinder model. The presented in 2011 Aventador car has been acclaimed by customers and journalists alike. The Lamborghini Aventador LP 700-4's technology package is unique. It's structure for the cabin, body and chassis is based on an innovative monocoque made from the carbon fiber reinforced polymers that combine the systematic lightweight design with the optimum stiffness and safety. The new twelve-cylinder car engine with a total displacement(engine size) of the 6.5 liters and 700 bhp (515 kW) of the engine's power combines the best in high rpm revving thrills with mighty pulling power. It's super-fast ISR transmission, permanent all-wheel drive and push-rod suspension combine this potent power with the best safe handling precision.

The Aventador J benefits enormously and naturally, from this unique technology package. Yet the Aventador J has a significantly different interpretation to the Aventador coupe. The monocoque has a largely new design including the two safety bars behind the seats in this open version. The car design features like the absence of a roof, large windshield, of the air-conditioning system, navigation system obviously takes it's weight to an even lower lever. With a dry weight of the only 1575 kilograms, the series production Aventador LP 700-4 is already extremely light for its performance class thanks to its carbon fiber construction. The unique expertise of the Automobili Lamborghini company in field of carbon fiber reinforced polymers is evident not only in the hi-tech monocoque, but also in the research into the many further innovative solutions. The seats in the Aventador J are made of the Forged COMPOSITE, with inserts of flexible carbon fiber fabrics as the result of an innovative Lamborghini patent unlike traditional seats. The specialists at Lamborghini have developed an even more amazing version of the carbon fiber material for the Aventador J sports car. In its first automotive application, this carbon fiber fabric called "Carbonskin" is made of the woven carbon fibers soaked with a very special epoxy resin that stabilizes the fiber structure and keeps the material soft. Like a hi-tech fabric, the carbon fiber mats fit perfectly to every shape. The complete cockpit and parts of the seats in this car are made in this material and shimmer in matt carbon fiber black. It's conceivable that in future there will be many potential applications for this freshly patented and the extremely fine-looking material, even for making the very high-end clothing. An extreme sports car obviously needs an equally single-minded function and aerodynamic car design, which goes without saying at the Centro Stile by the Lamborghini.

This functionality is very clearly defined for this sports Aventador J car. It delivers the explosive dynamics, extreme driving fun, a unique experience. Virtually every part of the outer chassis was redesigned for the Aventador J. Yet it also shows the spirit of Lamborghini in most concentrated form. The car's dimensions are extreme: the overall length is 4890 mm, the overall width (excluding mirrors) is 2030 mm while the height is 1110 mm. The highest points are marked by the rear view mirror, which is perched on an arm like a periscope, and by the two safety bars behind the seats. There are two small wind deflectors in place of the classic front windshield. The occupants of the Aventador J are confronted by the Nature's element like the wind in much the same way as the racing car drivers in the Formula 1 competition .The front end of the Aventador J car looks like a Formula 1 racing car while viewed from the side. The significantly wider style elements and the rear diffuser form a perfect contrast to body paintwork. The special red color was developed specifically for this car. This is highly intensive red color with slight chrome effect. The wheels were also developed specifically for this car with the 20-inch rims at the front axle and 21-inch at the rear end. The five-spoke aluminum wheels have a central lock system and an additional carbon fiber insert that functions just like a small fan for optimum brake ventilation. The doors on the Aventador J car also open upward. They are considerably thinner than on the Aventador coupe and are fitted with a tiny, fixed side window. The muscular flanks around the rear wheels are hallmark Lamborghini and make it immediately apparent where this particular bull keeps his power.

The rear end consists in principle of just three elements: the carbon-fiber rear diffuser, the four huge tail pipes and the rear lights with their typical Lamborghini light signature in the form of a capital letterY.   The remaining surface area is for heat dissipation and is enclosed only by black metal mesh. The rear end is crowned by an large fixed spoiler mounted on the body shell by two arms.   The spoiler is supported by two pillars connected by the diffuser. Such design is clearly inspired by racing.   The exclusive Aventador J car has the special front and rear bumpers in the difference with the Aventador LP 700-4 car.   The both bumpers have been supplemented with the special carbon fiber fins that act as the flow deviators. Their purpose is to achieve a significant increase in the vehicle's down force at both the front and the rear axle.   The engine cover also brings the inside function to the outside.   It is not so much a cover but more a chassis framework to be more precise. This part has a new geometry (X shape) and is made of carbon fiber. Two large openings lay bare both cylinder banks of the mighty V12 power unit with it's 6.5 liters of displacement.   The Aventador J's car exterior and interior forms flow seamlessly into each other. This band of color connects the front and the rear of the car, creates a visual separation between the driver and passenger space and is interrupted only by a control panel housing for the starter button and switches for lights and transmission. The Aventador J is not equipped with a navigation GPS and car audio system. It does not have the associated screen or air-conditioning controls. These would simply detract from it's the one and only main function as an driving experience. There are two programmable TFT displays just behind the steering wheel.

2012 Lamborghini Aventador J
Car Performance Specifications

Engine Size	6.5Liter (396.8 inch)
Engine Power	692BHP(515KW)@8250rpm
Engine Torque	509ft-lbs(690 Nm)@5500rpm
Redline RPM	8500 rpm
Transmission	7-Semi-automatic
Gearbox	7-speed manual
Clutch	Twin Disc Clutch
Drive Wheels	All Wheels Drive, AWD
Car Weight	1300 kg (2870 lbs)
Acceleration time 0-60 mph	2.5 sec.
Acceleration time 0-60 kmph	1.7 sec.
Acceleration time 0-100 mph	5.3 sec.
Acceleration time 0-100 kmph	2.7 sec.
Quarter Mile time and speed	10 sec.@141 mph
Maximum Skidpad	1.3g
Maximum Top Speed	354 kmph (220 mph)
Braking to complete stop , 60-0 mph	121 ft
Maximum Slalom Speed	62 mph
Fuel Economy Miles Per Gallon	5/10 (city/hwy)

2012 Lamborghini Aventador J

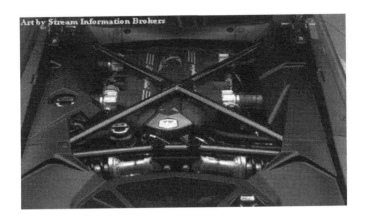

Car Engine Specifications

Manufacturer	Automobili Lamborghini S.p.A.
Design	60 degrees V12
Location	Middle/Longitudinally
Materials	Aluminum block, heads
Size	6.5Liter (396.8 cubic inch)
Max. Power	692BHP(515KW)@8250rpm
Max. Torque	509ft-lbs(690 Nm)@5500rpm
Max. RPM	8500 rpm
Bore, Stroke	95.0mm (3.7 in), 76.4mm (3.0 in)
Compression	11.8 : 1
Valvetrain	DOHC, 4 valves per cylinder
Fuel	Petrol (gasoline)
Fuel Delivery	Fuel injection
Aspiration	Naturally Aspirated
Ignition System	Electronic

2012 Lamborghini Aventador
Car Technical Specifications

Body mfgr   Automobili Lamborghini S.p.A.
Body Design   Monocoque
Body Style   2 Door Coupe
Body Materials   Carbon Fiber, Aluminum
Engine mfgr   Automobili Lamborghini S.p.A.
Engine Size   6.5Liter(396.8 cubic inch)
Transmission   7-Speed Semi-automatic
Gearbox   7-speed manual
Clutch   Twin Disc Clutch
Drive Wheels   ALL Wheels Drive, AWD
Chassis Design   Monocoque body w/ Front
and Rear Aluminum
Subframes
Chassis Materials   Carbon Fibre, Aluminum
Front Suspension Double Wishbones w/Pushrod
Operated   Shock Absorbers
Rear Suspension   Double Wishbones w/Pushrod
Operated Shock Absorbers
Car Steering   Rack & Pinion w/Power Assist
Car Front Brakes   Carbon Ceramic Discs
w/Brembo 8-Piston Calipers
Car Rear Brakes   Carbon Ceramic Discs
w/Brembo 6-Piston Calipers

2012 Lamborghini Aventador J

2012 Lamborghini Aventador J

Art by Stream Information Brokers

Overall Car Specifications

Car Length	4890 mm (192.5 in)
Car Width	2030 mm (79.9 in)
Car height	1110 mm (43.7 in)
Car Weight	1300 kg (2870 lbs)
Car wheelbase	2700 mm (106.3 in)
Front wheels track	1750 mm (68.9 in)
Rear wheels track	1650 mm (65.0 in)
Front Wheels	10.0 in x 19 in
Rear Wheels	13.5 in x 20 in
Front Wheel Tires	255/35 ZR 19
Rear Wheel Tires	335/30 ZR 20

2005 LeBlanc Mirabeau

General Information

Country of Origin	Switzerland
Manufacturer	Leblanc cars
Parent Company	Wysstec GmbH
Chassic Numbers	----------
Number of Built cars	3
Years of production	2005
First display at	2005 Viena Motor Show
Mass Produced Model	----------
Asked Price:	478,000.00 Euros

Prices above are Manufacturers Suggested Retail Price
and could be different from auction or dealer prices!

2005LeBlanc Mirabeau
New Features in Car Design

You should be already very surprised to see the sports supercar made in the Switzerland among these Top10 world fastest exotic cars. Usually everybody knows about the top quality of the watches and the famous multifunction army knifes made in Switzerland. This small country in the middle of West Europe does not have any large car manufacturers. They are importing most of cars and trucks from France, Germany and Italy.   Just because of this you could rank very high this remarkable achievement by small unknown company almost on their own!   The Le Blanc Mirabeau is the newest car from the Wysstec GmbH and Leblanc cars. This is the real piece of art with the spirit of race that already prepared to satisfy the FIA and Le Mans race standards. And the Leblanc Mirabeau car really belongs on the racing track with this kind of potential. It is almost unbelievable to accept the fact that it is legal to drive car on the streets. The car has unique open cockpit body design made similar to the Formula 1 racing cars design.   The car gets the great aerodynamics with the middle of the car located engine and lowered as possible driver and passenger seats. The car body and car chassis made from lightweight materials to achieve the really large engine power to car's weight ratio and reach the top possible speeds with the best engine available for the unknown small company. The engine's power comes from the same V8 engine found in the CCR car manufactured by the small Sweden car manufacturer Koenigsegg.
It is equipped with a Lysholm Screw Compressor, which has several advantages to the common centrifugal compressor.

It creates a higher boost-pressure at lower rpm, thus increasing both acceleration and control at low speed. The lag times during shifts and on-off throttling are also reduced to a minimum. Nobody expects from the very small company in Switzerland to redesign or greatly impove the engine or any other components of the power train and the drivetrain. To reach the maximum of the lightweight in the car building and race feeling the car interior is optimized for maximum of speed and acceleration. There are some special options including the leather interior and a semi-automatic sequential gearbox.

2005LeBlanc Mirabeau
Car Performance Specifications

Engine Size   4.7 Liter (286.8 Cubic inch)
Engine Power   806BHP (601 KW)@6900 rpm
Engine Torque   679ft-lbs(920 Nm)@5700rpm
Redline RPM   7600 rpm
Transmission   Cima 6-Speed sequential
Gearbox   6-speed manual
Clutch   Twin Disc Clutch
Drive Wheels   Rear Wheels Drive, RWD
Car Weight   812kg (1790 lbs)
Acceleration time 0-60 mph   3.5 sec.
Acceleration time 0-60 kmph   2.7 sec.
Acceleration time 0-100 mph   8.1 sec.
Acceleration time 0-100 kmph   3.7 sec.
Quarter Mile time and speed   9.0 sec. @146 mph
Maximum Skidpad   1.3g
Maximum Top Speed   370   kmph (220mph)
Braking to complete stop , 60-0 mph   120 ft
Maximum Slalom Speed   77.1 mph
Fuel Economy Miles Per Gallon 10/17 (city/hwy)

2005LeBlanc Mirabeau

Car Engine Specifications

Manufacturer	Koenigsegg Automotive AB
Model	Koenigsegg CCR
Design	90 degrees V8
Location	Mid -engine, longitudinally
Materials	Aluminum block, heads
Size	4.7 Liter(286.8 cubic inch)
Max. Power	806BHP(601 KW)@6900rpm
Max. Torque	679ft-lbs(920 Nm)@5700rpm
Max. RPM	7600 rpm (redline)
Bore, Stroke	90.6mm(3.6 in), 92mm(3.62 in)
Compression	8.6 :1
Valvetrain	DOHC, 4 Valves per Cylinder
Fuel	Petrol (Gasoline)
Fuel Delivery	Fuel Injection
Aspiration	Supercharged
Ignition System	Electronic

2005LeBlanc Mirabeau
Car Technical Specifications

Body mfgr	LeBlanc Cars
Body Design	Monocoque
Body Style	2 Door Coupe
Body Materials	Carbonfiber, Aluminum
Engine mfgr	Koenigsegg Automotive AB
Engine Size	4.7Liter (286.1 cubic inch)
Transmission	Cima 6-Speed sequential
Gearbox	6-speed manual
Clutch	Twin Disc Clutch
Drive Wheels	Rear Wheels Drive, RWD
Chassis Design	Monocoque body w/ Front and Rear Aluminum Subframes,
Chassis Materials	Carbon Fibre, Aluminum
Front Suspension	Double Wishbones w/Pushrod Operated Shock Absorbers
Rear Suspension	Double Wishbones w/Pushrod Operated Shock Absorbers
Car Steering	Rack & Pinion w/Power Assist
Car Front Brakes	Carbon Ceramic Discs w/Brembo 8-Piston Calipers
Car Rear Brakes	Carbon Ceramic Discs w/Brembo 6-Piston Calipers

2005LeBlanc Mirabeau

Art by Stream Information Brokers

2005LeBlanc Mirabeau

Art by Stream Information Brokers

Overall Car Specifications

Car Length	4550 mm (179.1 in)
Car Width	2000 mm (78.7 in)
Car height	980 mm (38.6 in)
Car Weight	812 kg (1790 lbs)
Car wheelbase	2800 mm (110.2 in)
Front wheels track	1733 mm (68.2 in)
Rear wheels track	1682 mm (66.2 in)
Front Wheels	10.5 in x 19in
Rear Wheels	12.5 in x 19in
Front Wheel Tires	255/35 -R19
Rear Wheel Tires	305/30 -R19

2005 Saleen S7 twin turbo

General Information

Country of Origin	USA
Manufacturer	Saleen Inc.
Parent Company	--------
Chassic Numbers	--------
Number of Built cars	11
Years of production	2005
First display 2005 Los Angeles Auto Show	
Mass Produced Model	Saleen S7
Asked Price:	$555,000.00

Prices above are Manufacturers Suggested Retail Price
and could be different from auction or dealer prices!

2005Saleen S7 twin turbo
New Features in Car Design

The Saleen Inc. is one of the small group exotic car manufacturers to join the Ferrari, Bugatti, Maserati in close results competition to build the fastest sports cars with the highest top speeds and largest engines for best performance specification results. There is no exotic car manufacturer that would deal with new designs for their extreme super cars without new design and better aerodynamics for car body similar to design of the racing cars from Formula1, GrandPrix, Le Mans racing events. It is because the best aerodynamic would greatly reduce the air resistance and losses of engine power to fight the air friction against car body resistance. An aerodynamics had to play it most important role for performance of 2005 Saleen S7 Twin Turbo. This new 2005 extreme super car has a different diffuser/rear spoiler package and reshaped front fenders to improve already a good car aerodynamics. The redesigned front and rear diffusers, along with the new rear spoiler, had reduced aero drag (air friction resistance) on 40 percent and a have got the car the 60 percent increase in the down force. And engine power and torque figures are looked spectacular at 750 horsepower and 700 lb-ft of the torque. Saleen engineers have performed well with the redesign of the original S7's 7-liter engine in order to get such increase in engine output! That would be impossible without using the Twin Turbo's enhanced straight-line performance envelope. The new all-aluminum V8 engine casting was engineered and tooled by Saleen to displace the engine size in seven liters.

All new engine design includes stainless steel valves, titanium retainers, beryllium exhaust valve seats, an aluminum throttle body, Saleen-designed aluminum CNC-machined cylinder heads and stainless steel exhaust system. The unique V8 engine has a unique Saleen-designed side-mounted water pump, a belt-driven camshaft drive and a Saleen-engineered dry sump oil delivery system. The engine's original mid-chassis location optimizes weight distribution and makes room for an unusually tall and very efficient engine intake induction system similar to Formula1 racing cars.

The air enters a roof intake, passes through a 90-mm mass air meter and feeds into a carbon fiber plenum. The air needed to mix with fuel is routed from the plenum to the twin ball bearing turbos. This is pressurized air to 5.5 psi max and then passes through an oval-bore throttle body into an aluminum intake manifold with eight individual cylinder air intake flow passages. The new car fuel injection system includes dual electric fuel pumps and high-capacity, return-less, 52 lb/hr fuel injectors. The dual or twins the twotwin-ball-bearing, water-cooled Saleen-Garrett turbos with 44-mm wastegates are designed integrated into the S7's stainless steel high-flow exhaust system. The four exhaust pipes from each bank of cylinders merge into a race-car-like high-efficiency collector. In addition, the exhaust incorporates dual catalysts per cylinder bank, EGR and those mentioned twin wastegates.

This extreme exotic Saleen car comes prepared for regular road use with the emission control system features dual, heated oxygen sensors per cylinder bank and a high-volume evaporative emission system along with those four catalysts. All fuel system is OBD-II compliant. The design of a high rpm speed engine with the turbochargers the needed to use the solid lifters instead of hydraulic lifters. Saleen engineers also added oil squirters into engine lubrication system to provide the additional cooling to the undersides of the pistons. This new extreme Saleen car has the new-generation six-speed transaxle, with a unique Saleen bell housing, transfers power to the wheels. The clutch is an organic/metallic 8.0-inch, twin-plate unit with the hydraulic actuation. The chassis of the regular S7 has to be also redesigned in order to fit well with all the extreme car high performance packages. The suspension geometry has been modified for more stability in handling and less squat and dives during acceleration and braking. This major improvement in a ride is done with the use the dual-stage design suspension coil springs. The second stiffer springs start coming into play at around 100 mph with the car developing the serious downforce. The shocks in suspension of a new car chassis have the revised shock valving for front and rear of the car!

This new extreme car was outfitted with new the Saleen-engineered and the Brembo-supplied lightweight aluminum six-piston mono-block calipers for the front and rear disk car brakes. The brakes has15-inch vented discs up front and 14-inch vented discs at the rear. The S7 Twin Turbo car incorporates a revised pedal box. The clutch and the throttle lever ratios pedals have been changed for lighter pedal efforts. In addition, the three pedals have been spaced farther apart without impinging upon the dead pedal. This is adding to better car ergonomics for the driver!

2005Saleen S7 twin turbo
Car Performance Specifications

Engine Size	7.0Liter (427 cubic inch)
Engine Power	750BHP(559KW)@6300 rpm
Engine Torque	700ft-lbs(949 Nm)@4800 rpm
Max RPM	6500 rpm (redline)
Transmission	6-Speed Manual
Gearbox	6-speed manual
Clutch	Twin Disc Clutch
Drive Wheels	Rear Wheels Drive, RWD
Car Weight	1338 kg (2950 lbs)
Acceleration time 0-60 mph	2.8 sec.
Acceleration time 0-60 kmph	2.3 sec.
Acceleration time 0-100 mph	6.0 sec.
Acceleration time 0-100 kmph	3.0 sec.
Quarter Mile time and speed	10.7 sec.@136mph
Maximum Skidpad	1.1g
Maximum Top Speed	160 mph
Braking to complete stop , 60-0 mph	147 ft
Maximum Slalom Speed	73 mph
Fuel Economy Miles Per Gallon	10/15 (city/hwy)

2005Saleen S7 twin turbo

Car Engine Specifications

Manufacturer	Saleen Inc.
Design	V8
Location	Mid-engine/Longitudinally
Materials	Aluminum Head , Block
Size	7.0Liter (426.6 cubic inch)
Max. Power	750HP(559.3KW)@6300rpm
Max. Torque	700ft-lbs(949Nm)@4800rpm
Max. RPM	6500 rpm (redline)
Bore, Stroke	105mm(4.12 in), 102mm(4.0 in)
Compression	10.8 : 1
Valvetrain	OHV, 2 Valves per Cylinder
Fuel	Petrol(Gasoline)
Fuel Delivery	Fuel injection
Aspiration	Twin Garrett GT35R Turbos
Ignition System	Electronic

2005Saleen S7 twin turbo
Car Technical Specifications

Body mfgr   Saleen Inc.

Body Design   Honeycomb, Steel Frame

Body Style   2 Door Coupe

Body Materials Carbonfiber, Aluminum

Engine mfgr   Saleen Inc.

Engine Size   7.0Liter (426.6 cubic inch)

Transmission   6-Speed Manual

Gearbox   6-speed manual

Clutch   Twin Disc Clutch

Drive Wheels   Rear Wheels Drive, RWD
with Limited Slip Differential

Chassis Design   Steel Space Frame

Chassis Materials Carbon Fibre, Aluminum,
Plastic, Steel

Front Suspension Unequal Double Wishbones
w/Coil-OverAluminum
Dampers, Anti-Roll Bar

Rear Suspension Unequal Double Wishbones
w/Coil-OverAluminum
Dampers, Anti-Roll Bar

Car Steering   Rack & Pinion w/Power Assist
Michelin Pilot Sport PS2

Car Front Brakes   Brembo Ventilated Discs
w/6-Piston Calipers

Car Rear Brakes   Brembo Ventilated Discs
w/6-Piston Calipers

2005Saleen S7 twin turbo

2005Saleen S7 twin turbo

Art by Stream Information Brokers

Overall Car Specifications

Car Length	4774 mm (188.0 in)
Car Width	1990 mm (78.3 in)
Car height	1041 mm (41.0 in)
Car Weight	1338 kg (2950 lbs)
Car wheelbase	2700 mm (106.3 in)
Front wheels track	1748 mm (68.8 in)
Rear wheels track	1710 mm (67.3 in)
Front Wheels	9.5 in x 19 in
Rear Wheels	12.5 in x 20 in
Front Wheel Tires	275/35 -R19 Michelin
Rear Wheel Tires	335/30 -R20 Michelin

About this Book

Description

Finally the first in the world one of kind unique ultimate spectacular book on currently 10 Best World Fastest Most Expensive High Performance Exotic Cars inside this Best Desktop Exclusive Reference Encyclopedia Guide with the never published in one publication the articles, unique data and info, cars' pictures, all major technical, performance and overall specifications for each of those Rare Exotic cars owned by richest car collectors, billionaires, world top royalty and top Hollywood and pro sports superstars celebrities is here. Your Major Benefits from ownership of this sensational book!
- By Now You should completely Relax,Have Summer Fun! Let this fantastic book to make You more cool, hot and popular than ever before with more success in networking, socialising with cars and racing fans.
- Or simply turn this Sensational book into Perfect Gift for any personal, business, corporate holiday,event or ocassion. OtherYour Benefits from Buying this Sensational Book!
- Easy to find in 1(one) book all data, specs for 10 different cars from different car manufacturers intead of wasting days, months looking through 1000 Web and print sources.
-Fastest way to learn about Top achievements of automotive industry straight from Top Automotive Experts.
-Most Simple Best Reference Guide on World Top10 Best Fastest Muscle Supercars for car racing fans, car collectors, students, cars experts.
- Cheapest Way to get Top Expertise on Cars instead of the buying info from 1000 self -proclaimed as "Cars Experts" and self-published at thousands Web and print sources.

Book Title

10 Best World Fastest Most Expensive Rare Exotic Cars.

Book subtitle

Best Sensational Unique Desktop Ultimate
One of Kind Reference Guide with Unique
Never Previously seen in One Publication
Pictures, Major Technical and Performance
Specifications for 10 World Best Exotic
Muscle Preformance Street Sport Cars.

Keywords

Book Best Cars, Book Top Cars, Book Exotic Cars,
World Best Cars, Top10 Sports Cars, Best Racing Cars,
Top Performance Cars, World Fastest Cars, World Expensive
Cars, Book Fastest Cars, Book Expensive Cars, World Exotic
Cars, Book 10 Best Cars, Ferrari, Bugatti, Lamborghini,
Maserati, Mclaren, Koenigsegg, Pagani, 10 Best Cars, Top10
Best Cars, Street Racing Cars, Top10 Exotic Cars, Top
Muscle Cars, Best Exotic Cars, Best Fastest Cars, Best
Expensive Cars, Best Preformance Cars, Best Sports Cars,
Best Racing Cars, Exotic Cars, Fastest Cars, Racing Cars,
Sports Cars, Sports Super Cars, Super Cars, Best Supercars,
Best Cars, Muscle Cars, Top10 Cars, Top10 Best Cars,
Top10 Fastest Cars, Most Expensive Cars , Classic Cars,
Rare Cars, Super Cars, Formula1 Cars, Rare Collector's Cars,
Collector's Cars.

About Author

The author of this Awesome book is Mr. Roman Slepyan. He is the well-known top expert on everything about the cars including cars' design, engines's design, cars' performance, engines' performance, cars' and trucks' manufacturing, cars' and trucks' testing, automotive engineering, cars' service and repair, cars' marketing and sales.

Mr. Roman Slepyan had founded the 1Best Car Buyer Club Ask Top Experts Network in order to offer the exclusive help by the Top experts professionals for the Cars', Trucks', SUVs', vans' buyers, owners, drivers to deal with all their car problems and troubles. He with the group of other Top experts on other types of the modern transportation like the aircrafts, planes, boats, yachts, rockets, space shuttles had founded World Best Exotics Classifieds Online Magazine (http://1bestclassifieds.freeservers.com) to share the Top expertise and provide the big help for the amateurs and the professionals to promote, advertise their causes, businesses, opportunities, races, shows, events. Mr. Roman Slepyan is one of the founders for the Stream Information Brokers company (www.streaminfobrokers.com) - one of the first official information brokerage firms in the world. He is also one of founders for the 1NewsPortal (www.1newsportal.com) as unique one of kind ultimate and Best reference directory on news by the Top experts on all possible specific subjects and topics. Mr. Roman Slepyan is the Degreed professional automotive design engineer expert with 30 years of hands-on experience and professional expertise. He participated in the latest high performance cars' and car engines' designs, the car aerodynamics theory and design, the prototypes' cars design and manufacturing, new top high performance and race cars and trucks test drives.

Page120

Book Review

Finally just published the first in the world one of kind unique best desktop one stop ultimate reference guide on the Top10 World Best Fastest Most Expensive Exotic Cars of the 20th century with never published in one publication the pictures, all major technical data, performance specifications. You will get the Instant Quick, Easy Recognition, Reward, Gratification and Popular boy or girl Status for competence and knowledge about these Top10 cars with this compact Encyclopedia on the world best cars book. It is very Easy now to find in this 1(one) book all data, specs for all 10 different cars from different car manufacturers instead of wasting days, months looking through the thousands Web and print sources. You get here on Fastest way to learn about the Top Cars and automotive industry straight from the top best automotive experts. This book is the most simple best reference guide on the world's best Top10 fastest most expensive exotic cars for car racing fans, car collectors, students, cars' experts. Now You can take with this book the cheapest way to get the top expertise on cars instead of buying similar info from the thousands self -proclaimed as "cars' experts" the web, print sources.

Message from the publisher
Stream Information Brokers

You invited to Place ads in World Exotics Best Classifieds Online Magazine (http://1bestclassifieds.freeservers.com) to sell your muscle car or promote the local exotic, rare sports and muscle car owners' club event! Ask Top experts the questions about cars or To find out more specific reference or news by experts professionals on the any car by visiting the Mobile ASE Mechanics website online at this URL address (http://mechanicsase.tripod.com). Get now online 24-7 the best latest complete top muscle cars desktop reference and expertise primary resources with your membership to the 1Best Top Reference News Directory at this URL address (www.1newsportal.com). Ask the top business, marketing, sales experts from Stream Information Brokers company at (www.streaminfobrokers.com) to help your muscle car dealer business or muscle car owners' club to organize and handle the different business, marketing, sales, PR publicity Events! Stream info Brokers has best experts on the marketing and advertising to offer you the help to do much better, cheaper, faster, more simple and easy all marketing, advertising, promotions,sales! Stream info Brokers has best experts on the packaging and distribution for the your internet video products, digital information products, digital multimedia products, electronic info products. Such products could be packaged for download, distribute via email messages as attachments, view and sharing on the web, packaged as software, packaged as DVD for street distribution. We are manufacturing some simple Animated Video with Sound promotional products. The samples of those products are available at company website -www.streaminfobrokers.com.

About Publisher

The publisher of this amazing book Stream Information Brokers company is in business to provide the small, large and middle size businesses also individuals with the priceless help in the promoting their professionalism, expertise, products, services through the affordable Best Marketing, Advertising, Promotions, Sales and Management problem solving complete solutions and stand-alone campaigns.
We are the Major Providers of Latest Top Expertise, Best References, Best Human Knowledge Resources, Always Best Money Making and Life Saving Info, Insider Secrets, Tips, Tricks for Your Success, Fame and Fortune at time when you need it most!